NATIVE AMERICANS IN TEXAS

Janey Levy

Published in 2010 by The Rosen Publishing Group, Inc.
29 East 21st Street, New York, NY 10010

Book Design: Michael J. Flynn

Photo Credits: Cover (hunting scene) Charles Marion Russell/The Bridgeman Art Library/Getty Images; cover, pp. 3, 4, 6, 10, 14, 22, 24, 30, 31, 32 (Texas emblem on all), 3–32 (textured background), 12 (alligator), 14–15 (Caddo), 17 (bison), back cover (Texas flag) Shutterstock.com; pp. 5 (both petroglyphs), 7 (Galveston, Texas), 13 (Atakapa), 16 (pottery and village), 17 (figurine and shell),19 (Angelina River) Wikipedia Commons; pp. 6 (Cabeza de Vaca), 16 (preparing meal) MPI/Hulton Archive/Getty Images; p. 9 (pueblo) George Eastman House/Hulton Archive/Getty Images; p. 8 (map) © GeoAtlas; pp. 11 (family), 27 (Quanah Parker) Hulton Archive/Getty Images; p. 21 (Native American) Paul J. Richards/AFP/Getty Images; p. 22 (Native American chief) George Eastman/Hulton Archive/Getty Images; p. 23 (desert) James L. Stanfield/ National Geographic/Getty Images; p. 25 (Geronimo) Hulton Archive/Getty Images; p. 25 (Native Americans around tepee) Popperfoto/Getty Images; p. 26 (Comanches) Frederic Lewis/Hulton Archive/Getty Images; p. 28 (Kiowa boy) Will Soule/Time & Life Pictures/Getty Images.

Library of Congress Cataloging-in-Publication Data

Levy, Janey.
Native Americans in Texas / Janey Levy.
    p. cm. — (Spotlight on Texas)
Includes index.
  ISBN 978-1-61532-451-4 (pbk.)
  ISBN: 978-1-61532-487-3 (6-pack)
  ISBN 978-1-61532-488-0 (library binding)
1. Indians of North America—Texas—History—Juvenile literature. 2. Indians of North America—Texas—
Social life and customs—Juvenile literature. I. Title.
E78.T4L53 2010
976.404'97—dc22
                        2009049058

Manufactured in the United States of America

CPSIA Compliance Information: Batch # WW1ORC: For further information contact Rosen Publishing, New York, New York at 1-800-237-9932.

CONTENTS

TEXAS BEFORE THE EXPLORERS CAME 4

SPANISH EXPLORERS AND   6
   NATIVE AMERICANS

NATIVE AMERICANS OF THE   10
   GULF COAST

EAST TEXAS TRIBES   14

SOUTH TEXAS TRIBES   22

NATIVE AMERICANS OF CENTRAL   24
   AND WEST TEXAS

READER RESPONSE PROJECTS   30

GLOSSARY   31

INDEX   32

Texas Before the Explorers Came

What do you imagine when you think of Texas history? People often think first of European **explorers**, then the Battle of the Alamo and Texas's fight for independence. Yet European explorers weren't the first people in Texas. When they arrived, about 30,000 Native Americans were living there. Their **ancestors** had come to the area more than 10,000 years earlier!

The earliest people got their food by hunting wild animals and gathering wild plants and nuts. They ate things like buffalo, rabbits, squirrels, and snakes. They moved often as they searched for food. Some camped in open areas. Others lived in caves. Later, groups living in areas with good soil began farming. The lives of all these people changed forever when Spanish explorers arrived in the early 1500s.

Ancient people in Texas often painted on or cut pictures into rocks. Common subjects were people, animals, the sun, weather, trees, and hunting and fighting tools. You can still see these ancient pictures at more than 250 places in Texas.

SPANISH EXPLORERS AND NATIVE AMERICANS

Explorer Álvar Núñez Cabeza de Vaca gave the first reports of Native Americans in Texas. In 1528, Cabeza de Vaca landed on an island near the Texas coast. He lived among Native Americans for about 8 years and later wrote about his adventures. He said the Native American groups—the Capoques and the Hans—were very tall and strong. They decorated their bodies by poking holes in their skin and putting sticks through them. They wore few clothes, lived in tents, and were **nomads**. They ate fish, roots, **oysters**, blackberries, pecans, prickly pear cactus fruits, deer, buffalo, and even lizards, snakes, rats, and spiders!

Álvar Núñez Cabeza de Vaca

Cabeza de Vaca was born in a small Spanish village around 1490. During his years with the Native Americans, he became a trader and healer. He also learned great respect for the people and their ways of life. He died in Spain around 1555.

Álvar Núñez Cabeza de Vaca and about 60 others landed near Galveston Island. This picture shows Galveston today.

Cabeza de Vaca also wrote about other coastal groups, or tribes: the Charrucos, Quevenes, Yguases, Deguenes, Guaycones, and Quitoles. All these tribes lived much like the Capoques and Hans did.

Later—between 1540 and 1542—Francisco Coronado traveled through the **Panhandle** of northwestern Texas. While searching for cities of gold that Native Americans had reported, Coronado and his men met Apaches. They also met Kiowas, Tejas, and Zuni. Does the name "Tejas" look familiar? It should. Texas got its name from the Tejas. "Tejas" comes from the east Texas Caddo tribe's word for "friend."

Around the time of Coronado's trip, Luis de Moscoso Alvarado led a group of Spanish explorers into eastern Texas. Moscoso and his men were the first Europeans to meet the Caddo and Hasinai tribes of that area.

This 1873 picture shows the Zuni pueblo in New Mexico. In 1540, Coronado and about 200 of his men attacked a nearby pueblo, looking for the "Seven Cities of Gold."

Native Americans of the Gulf Coast

Many of the coastal tribes Cabeza de Vaca wrote about died from illnesses brought by Spanish explorers. Those who lived may have been ancestors of the later Karankawas.

"Karankawa" was the name for several groups with a common language and **culture**. They reportedly raised dogs, and the name may mean "dog lovers."

The Karankawas painted and **tattooed** their bodies. They were nomadic hunters and gatherers who traveled by foot or canoe. They lived in tents, made baskets and clay dishes, and used bows and arrows. Karankawa men were strong fighters who enjoyed showing their strength and skill.

As more Europeans came, the Karankawas fought to drive them away. They also fought U.S. settlers who began coming in the early 1800s. The fighting ended in 1858, when Texans killed the last Karankawas.

Although no pictures of the Karankawas exist, pictures of other Native Americans of the time can help us understand them. This picture shows Native Americans of southern California who lived much like the Karankawas did. This traveling family even has a dog with them. Their clothes, however, are much different from those of the Karankawas.

Besides the Karankawas, there was another set of coastal groups called the Atakapas. The two groups looked very different. The Karankawas were tall and strong. The Atakapas were short, wide, and dark.

Like the Karankawas, the Atakapas were hunters and gatherers. An important animal for them was the alligator, which supplied meat, hides, and oil. You might think the oil was used for cooking and heating, but that's not true. The Atakapas rubbed the oil on their bodies to keep bugs from biting them!

alligator

The Atakapas were also traders. They traded with other Native American groups and with the Spanish and French. Because they dealt so much with the Europeans, many Atakapas caught European illnesses. In the end, the illnesses killed all the Atakapas.

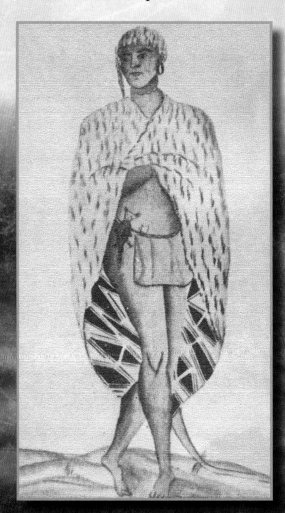

This 1735 painting shows an Atakapa Indian dressed for winter.

EAST TEXAS TRIBES

North of the Gulf Coast are the forests and rich soil of east Texas. The land and weather in east Texas is unlike the land and weather along the coast. Because of this, the tribes there had a different way of life.

The Caddos were an important east Texas tribe. "Caddo" is a short form of their full name, Kadohadacho, which means "real chiefs." Like the coastal tribes, they hunted. However, they farmed, too. Their major crop was corn, or maize. They also raised beans, squash, sunflowers, and pumpkins. They made tools and baskets, and were famous for their beautiful clay objects. To make clothes, they wove cloth from plant fibers. On special occasions, they wore clothes decorated with feathers. They also wore rings through their noses and covered their bodies with tattoos.

This is a modern-day Caddo. He is dressed much like his ancestors were hundreds of years ago.

From ancient times, the Caddos were also traders. They traded for goods from as far away as Canada! Some goods were so highly prized that they were buried with Caddo leaders and wealthy members of the tribe.

Since the Caddos weren't nomads, they lived in houses rather than tents. Their houses were made of poles covered by grass. At the center of a Caddo community was an earthen mound with a temple on top. Caddos also built earthen mounds for burying people.

The Caddos used baskets and clay dishes to prepare food and clay dishes for cooking, much like the Indians shown here.

This is an artist's idea of what a Caddo village might have looked like.

The Caddos made clay dishes in many shapes and sizes.

CADDOAN

Each Caddo village had several important leaders. There was a **religious** leader and a chief, or headman. The village also had a group of **elders**.

The Caddos believed in several gods. The chief god was Caddi Ayo, who was the creator.

The Caddos made small stone figures much like this one of a woman smashing corn.

Through trade, the Caddos got shells from coastal tribes. They decorated the shells with pictures.

The Caddos hunted buffalo for their fur and meat.

CULTURE

17

Another group of east Texas Native Americans were the Hasinais. They were closely connected to the Caddos and spoke a Caddoan language.

Like the Caddos, the Hasinais hunted and farmed. Their main crops were maize, beans, and squash. Their houses were much like Caddo houses. They also built temple and burial mounds. Each village had a religious leader, a chief, and elders, too. Their chief god was Caddi Ayo.

José María

José María was a chief of the Anadarkos, a Hasinai tribe. He was born around 1800 and likely died in the 1860s. At first, he fought the settlers moving onto Anadarko land. However, he soon realized there were too few Anadarkos to beat the settlers. He spent the rest of his life trying to make peace between the Anadarkos and settlers.

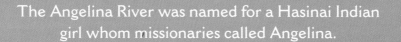
Angelina River

The Angelina River was named for a Hasinai Indian girl whom missionaries called Angelina.

In the 1700's, the Wichita, Alabamas, and Coushattas arrived in east Texas from other places. The Wichita called themselves Kitikiti'sh, or "raccoon eyes," because of the tattoos around the men's eyes. The Wichita were known for their tattoos. They were also famous for their friendliness to strangers.

Although the Alabamas and Coushattas were separate tribes, they were called the Alabama-Coushattas because they had lived together for centuries. They settled in a wooded area that had excellent hunting and gathering. The thick woods kept other people from bothering them. Both tribes lived in cabins. Groups of cabins connected by trails formed communities.

The 1700s Outside Texas

When the 1700s began, the United States didn't exist. England claimed most of the land along the Atlantic coast. Spain claimed Florida. England and France both claimed the land between the Appalachian Mountains and the Mississippi River. In 1754, they went to war over it. England won in 1763. It also got Florida from Spain that year. In 1775, the English colonies fought to gain their independence. They won in 1783, and the United States was born.

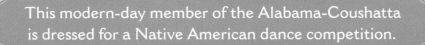

This modern-day member of the Alabama-Coushatta is dressed for a Native American dance competition.

SOUTH TEXAS TRIBES

Many different small tribes once lived in south Texas. Together, they're called Coahuiltecans. However, little is known about them, and it's not certain the tribes shared a language and culture.

Most Coahuiltecans were nomadic hunters and gatherers. The hot, dry area was one of the poorest parts of North America, and its tribes vanished early. Diseases and war killed some. Settlers and other Indians who moved into the area pushed out the others.

Cabeza de Vaca wrote about one south Texas tribe—the Mariames. He said they lived much like the coastal tribes.

In the 1800s, a band of Kickapoos settled in southwestern Texas. Settlers had forced them to leave their original home around the Great Lakes, and they became leaders in the fight to guard Native American land from settlers.

Kickapoo chief

This is the Chihuahuan Desert. It is part of Big Bend National Park in southwestern Texas.

Native Americans of Central and West Texas

Central and west Texas were home mostly to nomadic Plains tribes. They followed buffalo herds across the wide-open, flat land of the Great Plains. They ate buffalo meat, used the hides for clothes and tents, and made tools from the bones.

Cabeza de Vaca met Native Americans he called the "People of the Cows," who were likely Jumanos. They decorated their faces with tattooed or painted lines. They were among the first Indians to get horses, which were unknown before Spanish explorers came. By about 1700, the Apaches had destroyed Jumano culture.

Texas Apaches mostly belonged to the Lipan or Mescalero bands. Although they raised crops, they depended mostly on buffalo. Their skill on horseback made them powerful hunters and fighters. However, battles with Comanches and settlers weakened them. U.S. soldiers finally killed or captured all Texas Apaches in 1873.

Nomadic tribes lived in tepees like the one pictured. The Indians could easily carry the tepees with them as they moved from place to place.

Geronimo is a famous Apache leader and medicine man. He led his people in trying to save their lands and way of life.

Geronimo

The Comanches were a Plains tribe that reached Texas around 1750. Their name comes from a Ute Indian word meaning "enemy." They called themselves Nermernuh, which means "the people." They were outstanding riders whose skill made them great hunters and frightening enemies. Comanche society was **democratic**. They elected their leaders and allowed great individual freedom. They fought to keep settlers from taking their hunting land but were finally forced onto **reservations**.

Quanah Parker

Quanah Parker was the last great Comanche chief. He unsuccessfully fought to stop Texas settlers. He and his band were forced onto a reservation. There he helped them by backing education and new farming methods, and teaching them about white culture. He gained U.S. citizenship for everyone in his band. Quanah was born around 1845 and died in 1911.

This 1800 drawing shows a Comanche chief talking to members of his band.

In the early 1700s, several small Plains bands formed the Tonkawas. Sickness and war killed many. The rest joined other tribes. By about 1950, no Tonkawas remained.

The powerful Kiowas—also a Plains tribe—were hated and feared by their enemies. They were forced onto reservations in 1875. However, like Quanah Parker's band, they changed their ways and became U.S. citizens.

A small group of Tiguas from New Mexico settled near El Paso in the late 1600s. Today they live on a reservation near El Paso or in the city itself.

These are only some of the Native American tribes that once lived in Texas. The area was home to people with many different ways of life. Most of the tribes have vanished now, but they all helped shape Texas history.

NATIVE AMERICANS IN TEXAS

Coastal Tribes	Eastern Tribes	Southern Tribes	Central and Western Tribes
Capoques	Caddos	Coahuiltecans	Jumanos
Hans	Hasinais	Mariames	Apaches
Charrucos	Wichita	Kickapoos	Comanches
Quevenes	Alabamas		Tonkawas
Yguases	Coushattas		Kiowas
Deguenes			Tiguas
Guaycones			
Quitoles			
Karankawas			
Atakapas			

This picture of Lone Bear,
a Kiowa boy, was taken in 1870.

READER RESPONSE PROJECTS

- Read more about the tribes in this book. On poster board, create a timeline showing when each tribe first appeared in Texas. Write the date, the name of the tribe (including any other names they might be known by), and why they came.

- Choose one of the Texas tribes that vanished. Imagine that one of your ancestors belonged to this tribe. Use the library and the Internet to learn as much as you can about the tribe. Write a story telling what happened to the tribe and what the members of the tribe must have felt.

- Pick one of the following tribes: Caddos, Wichita, Alabama-Coushattas, Kickapoos, Apaches, Comanches, or Kiowa. Use the library and the Internet to learn as much as you can about the tribe's clothing and way of life. Then draw a picture showing a village or house of the tribe and include members of the tribe wearing their usual clothing.

GLOSSARY

ancestor (AN-sehs-tuhr) Someone in your family who lived long before you.

culture (KUHL-chur) The beliefs, practices, and goods of a group of people.

democratic (deh-muh-KRA-tihk) A way of life that gives all people a voice in how their society is run.

elder (EHL-duhr) A person who has authority because of their age and knowledge.

explorer (ihk-SPLOHR-uhr) A person who travels to new places to learn about them or search for riches.

nomad (NOH-mad) A person who moves from place to place as the seasons change in order to find food.

oyster (OYS-tuhr) A type of sea animal with a shell. People and many animals eat oysters.

Panhandle (PAN-han-duhl) A part of a state that sticks out from the rest of the state, somewhat like the handle of a pan.

religious (rih-LIH-juhs) Having to do with belief in a god or gods.

reservation (reh-zuhr-VAY-shun) An area of land set aside for Native Americans to live on.

tattoo (ta-TOO) The act of creating a picture or pattern on a person's skin by sticking color into the skin with needles. Also, the picture or pattern created this way.

Index

A

Alabama-Coushattas, 20, 30
Alabamas, 20, 29
Anadarko(s), 18
Apaches, 8, 24, 29, 30
Atakapas, 12, 13, 29

C

Cabeza de Vaca, Álvar
    Núñez, 6, 8, 10,
    22, 24
Caddi Ayo, 17, 18
Caddo(s), 8, 14, 16, 17, 18,
    29, 30
Capoques, 6, 8, 29
Charrucos, 8, 29
Coahuiltecans, 22, 29
Comanche(s), 24, 26, 27,
    29, 30
Coronado, Francisco, 8
Coushattas, 20, 29

D

Deguenes, 8, 29

G

Guaycones, 8, 29

H

Hans, 6, 8, 29
Hasinai(s), 8, 18, 29

J

José María, 18
Jumano(s), 24, 29

K

Karankawa(s), 10, 12, 29
Kickapoos, 22, 29, 30
Kiowas, 8, 28, 29, 30

L

Lipan, 24

M

Mariames, 22, 29
Mescalero, 24
Moscoso Alvarado, Luis de,
    8

P

Parker, Quanah, 27, 28
Plains tribe(s), 24, 26, 28

Q

Quevenes, 8, 29
Quitoles, 8, 29

T

Tejas, 8
Tiguas, 28, 29
Tonkawas, 28, 29

W

Wichita, 20, 29, 30

Y

Yguases, 8, 29

Z

Zuni, 8